THE MAN WHO LIVED
AMONG THE CANNIBALS

Cover Art:

Herman Melville, 1846.
Painting by Asa W. Twitchell. – Courtesy of the Berkshire Athenaeum.

American whaling ships at Kealakekua Bay, Hawaii, early 1840s.
Painting by whaler/artist Benjamin Russell, with Caleb Purrington,
1845, from their 1500-foot panorama, "Whaling Voyage Round
the World." – New Bedford Whaling Museum.

Cover Design: Jay Avila

Spinner Publications, Inc.
164 William Street
New Bedford, Massachusetts 02740

Library of Congress Cataloging-in-Publication Data

Robertson-Lorant, Laurie, 1940-
    The man who lived among the cannibals : poems in the voice of
Herman Melville / by Laurie Robertson-Lorant.
        p. cm.
    Includes bibliographical references.
    ISBN 0-932027-92-X (pbk.)
    1. Melville, Herman, 1819-1891—Poetry. 2. Authorship—
Poetry. 3. Authors—Poetry. I. Title.

PS3618.03175M36 2005
811'.6--dc22   2005011863

THE MAN WHO LIVED AMONG THE CANNIBALS

POEMS IN THE VOICE OF HERMAN MELVILLE

LAURIE ROBERTSON-LORANT

Spinner Publications, Inc.

New Bedford, Massachusetts

To my son Chris
and all who value kindness, justice, and diversity.

"My dear Sir, they begin to patronize. All fame is patronage.
Let me be infamous: there is no patronage in that. What
'reputation' H.M. has is horrible. Think of it! To go down to
posterity is bad enough, any way; but to go down as a 'man
who lived among the cannibals'! When I speak of posterity, in
reference to myself, I only mean the babies who will probably be
born in the moment immediately ensuing upon my giving up the
ghost. I shall go down to some of them, in all likelihood. 'Typee'
will be given to them, perhaps, with their gingerbread."

– Herman Melville to Nathaniel Hawthorne,
Arrowhead, May, 1851.

Contents

FOREWORD

"A Riddle to Unfold, A Wondrous Work in One Volume"
Laurie Robertson-Lorant's Poems in the Voice of Herman Melville

Sometime after finishing her dissertation on Melville and race at New York University in 1972, Laurie Robertson-Lorant realized there was much more to say about her subject. She found herself thinking beyond the scholarly confines of a dissertation to contemplate Melville himself—his encounters with diverse people outside the proper social circles of Albany and Boston, his interest in the wonders of nature, his response to personal tragedies, his ongoing interest in the possibilities of words. She began to explore these complicated dimensions in a few poems, recognizing that Melville was "a riddle to unfold, a wondrous work in one volume," as Ishmael describes Queequeg in *Moby-Dick*. When friends persuaded her that such unfolding would be possible only in a full-scale biography, Robertson-Lorant then began the arduous task of creating *Melville: A Biography*, which was published to great acclaim in 1996. Following the publication of this comprehensive and rich work, she returned to her poems, which gave her permission to do that which a formal biography forbids—to imagine and express Melville's own feelings in his own voice.

The Man Who Lived Among Cannibals might be considered a poetic memoir written in the first-person and arranged chronologically, beginning with Melville's reminiscences of his troubled boyhood and concluding with old age reveries on love and art. In her poems, Robertson-Lorant reveals her familiarity with the details of Melville's biography and of the history of his time as well as the details of his writings. Fusing her imagery with imagery from his works, she conveys the illusion of a personal intimacy with the depths of Melville's mind and heart.

Many of her poems reference *Moby-Dick*—the hardship of whaling, the mystery of the sea, the wonder of the whale. In "Melville at Twelve," she evokes Shakespeare's *The Tempest* to describe Melville's father's last days with an image of his being trapped in the tentacles of disease and debt, with young Herman's thought that he bobs free—a castaway— a reference to *Moby-Dick*'s Ishmael and Pip. To convey the appalling conditions on board American naval ships, in "Melville and George Orwell Take Refuge Inside the Whale," Robertson-Lorant brings together Melville's image in *White-Jacket* of sailors brutally flogged with the narrator's comment in *Mardi* that the red stripes on the flag look like the bloody gashes on the backs of American slaves. Cognizant of Melville's use of irony, satire, and puns to harpoon a point, Robertson-Lorant also enlivens his thoughts with witticisms, notably when "the problem of western philosophy, of course, / is that it puts Descartes before the horse" in "Melville Hitches Old Charlie to the Wagon."

By dramatizing Melville's real and imaginary meetings with figures from his own time, Robertson-Lorant establishes his social and historical dimensionality. She shows him in conversation with Frederick Douglass on the New Bedford docks as well as with Nathaniel Hawthorne on Monument Mountain and in Liverpool, and imagines him reflecting on his meeting with astronomer Maria Mitchell and overhearing the gossip that circulated about him in Pittsfield. In a moving "Interlude," she permits Melville's wife, Lizzie, to reveal the particulars of her disappointed romance with Herman. Robertson-Lorant also places her Melville outside the nineteenth century—in a powerful dialogue with George Orwell and in a series of pointed questions to Salman Rushdie—aligning their social criticism with his, and thereby vivifying his importance for our times.

In Robertson-Lorant's poems, although Melville speaks in various voices, she would have him consistently passionate—in his love, his defiance of oppression and injustice, his capacity to wonder, his struggle to continue writing in the face of rejection and indifference by contemporary critics. In her impersonation of him, Melville consistently and convincingly crosses boundaries—geographical, sexual, social, theological, philosophical, political. In "Melville in Judea," she writes with epigrammatic succinctness: "The true pilgrimage never ends. / It takes you over the edge / of the known world." And so, although Robertson-Lorant's poems bring us closer to a personal Melville, she tellingly shows us that he will always remain "a riddle to unfold, a wondrous work in one volume."

– Elizabeth Schultz, author of *Unpainted to the Last:*
Moby-Dick *and Twentieth Century American Art*

Herman Melville, an Aging Customs Inspector, Reminisces

Leaning against a dock-stump on Gansevoort Street
hunched in my woolen coat, walrus bagged in a double skin,
I shiver. In the harbor, the wind whines and whistles,
the masts creak like winter trees.

When I was a child, I would stand here for hours
watching sails swell toward the southern sky
as water lapped barnacle-encrusted pilings
that sprouted seaweed beards, medusa hair.

Inside the house, the furniture disappeared,
the rugs flew away—*to Araby*, Mother lied.
Floors froze like ice floes, and dampness
oozed from the basement like evil-smelling bilge.

Someday, I swore by my Father's mortgaged soul,
I will shoulder my duffel and sail forbidden seas,
far from the basilisk bankers and rat-faced creditors
gnawing at the corners of my room.

Someday I will sail to a land where work is play,
and poverty unknown: somewhere beyond
the shadow of the Fall—somewhere far from Manhattan,
that money-mad cannibal isle.

Melville at Twelve

Full fathom five
my father lies,
struggling to escape
the undertow.

Disease and debt
tighten their tentacles;
breaths bite
like barracudas.

He dives into death
defiant and insane,
and out of the maelstrom
I bob, a castaway.

Young Melville Crosses the Atlantic

On the voyage out, a sailor who had served
　　　on slave ships described to us almost gleefully
how they hauled "the filthy bastards" up on deck
　　　and tossed the dead ones overboard, then doused
the living with sea water to wash the vomit,
　　　excrement and blood from their naked bodies.
Then they herded the men back down into the hold
　　　and shackled them. Women, girls and boys
were kept on deck a while—unspeakably.

Melville in the Mother Country

Cargo offloaded, our packet-ship rides high
    beside the golden docks of Liverpool

as bales of cotton picked by Negro slaves
    await delivery to the textile mills.

The Mersey, an open sore, a filthy sewer,
    spits raw blood into the boiling sea.

At the base of a statue of Lord Nelson
    four captives in bronze manacles and chains

to represent the hero's naval victories
    huddle against the marble pedestal.

So pilot fish in the mid-Atlantic swim with sharks,
    the insatiable outriders of dark satanic ships.

Cabin-boy Melville Strolls through Liverpool

From an alley behind the cotton warehouses,
I heard feeble moans beneath a grate
and saw a gaunt woman with a bone-white baby

at her breast, a boy and girl huddled against her.
Holding out their hands to beg for food.
They cried for water. I could not meet their eyes.

I found a policeman. "It's not my beat," he growled.
The next morning, when the landlady wasn't looking,
I stole a few biscuits and a flask of tea.

As I lowered this meagre ration through the grate,
the children raised dirty hands and took the bread,
but the mother and bone-white baby never stirred.

The next morning, pockets stuffed with crusts,
I went back to the alley, but found no one there—
just a slurry of quicklime on the stones.

Melville on Lake Huron

Ojibway, Winnebago, Menominee
paddle birchbark canoes
in dignified silence, gliding by
wheezing steamboats. On the shore,
wigwams and crumbling fortresses
lend a kind of ancient grandeur
to the landscape beyond the towns
like Buffalo, where solemn chiefs
clad in blankets and buckskins
walk past newspaper offices,
courthouses, churches and hotels
listening to ghosts who whisper
old stories through the wind.

My ancestors came when
Algonkians were finding pearls
in New-York Harbor, when
Mohawks and Iroquois, Pequots,
Wampanoags, and Narragansetts
lived on sea coasts and islands,
in forests and fertile valleys
when the grass was green.
and the rivers ran fresh and clear.

Melville Stumbles into an African Meeting-House in New Bedford, Massachusetts

It was a December night without a moon—
just pinpricks of light from multitudes of stars,
and mounting the porch of what I thought
must be a tavern, or an inn, I kicked over
a box of ashes before opening the door.
Inside, a tall young man with curly hair
and copper skin was describing slavery—
the red-hot branding irons and galling chains,
the families torn apart by auctioneers.
In a voice of thunder, he vowed Almighty God
would punish the slaveholders for their sins,
and the congregation shouted, "Hallelujah!"—
"Praise the Lord!"—and "Amen!"

Just then, a gust of wind slammed shut the door,
and a hundred black faces turned and stared at me.
Flinging it open, I fled down the cobbled streets
wishing I could slough off whiteness
as easily as a snake can shed its skin.

Melville Meets a Stranger on New Bedford's Waterfront

Strolling at dusk along wharves
piled high with casks of oil,
I saw a man with the powerful physique
of a lion lately sprung from Africa

and recognized him by his thatch of hair
as the preacher who had compared
the abysmal darkness of Tophet
to the hell of slavery.

"Melville," I offered, holding out my hand.
The deep voice answered, "Douglass."

"The valiant Scot is one of my heroes," I replied,
hoping he might join me for a drink or two.

Just then a cold wind sliced across the pier,
and settling a tartan cap on his wild hair,
he bade me farewell and went back to his church
to continue fishing for the souls of men.

This handsome fellow became my silent partner
while I chased whales and sojourned
among tattooed savages who were more civilized
than we white cannibals will ever be.

Melville Heads for the Pacific Aboard the *Acushnet*

The ship's hull pounds and thumps against the waves;
after weeks of vomiting, greenhorns get sea legs.
Ice clinging to my eyebrows and my hair,
I lean against the railing in the wind
and watch the black bow cutting through the sea.

Fairhaven lies astern, and Lansingburgh:
the dead-end teaching jobs in country schools,
the sentimental poems and stories,
my Mother's relentless admonitions: "Be
sober, God-fearing, well-mannered, get a job,
and by all means, improve your handwriting;
people will judge you by your penmanship."

I climb the rigging and rock against the wind,
one hand on a halyard, one bare foot on a spar,
swinging the other arm and leg out free
to test who's stronger, me or gravity.

As we tack toward the Horn, the belles I wooed
with Byron and Tennyson seem far away.
In dreams, when I read poetry to girls,
they let me kiss them chastely on the cheek,
but in nightmares, they flounce angrily away,
and I wake up sweating, drenched in misery.

I imagine the chase, the thrust of the harpoon,
the straining muscles, the blinding spume and spray,
the maddened monster swimming for his life,
the wild careen through foaming, bloody seas.

All around, gray ocean and gray sky,
whitecaps like peaks of snow on every wave.
From my perch in the maintop, the black ship is a toy,
the sea, a dark and endless counterpane.

Melville Scans a Slate Sea

The sea is a mighty Gray,
each wave a fluke,
each crest a teasing spray.

As open ocean meets
a seamless sky,
the hull heaves and pitches

day after empty day,
and far beneath our keel
the great whales play.

Melville Arrives in the Marquesas

Brown breasts bobbing
    sleek bodies
        shiny hair

black tendrils
    undulating
        with the swell,

whihenies swim toward us
    like shoals of porpoises,
        their almond eyes, harpoons.

As we throw off our clothes
    and dive from the taffrail
        into the lagoon

seabirds shriek and clamor
    cold sharks
        cruise.

Melville Continues his Classical
Education in the South Seas

Banquet of buttocks, breasts and balls,
men and women naked except for shark-tooth
necklaces, feathers and tattoos that tempt
eye and hand to trace curves and contours,
men and women shamelessly aroused, arousing me
to big, bold bliss unknown in Puritan America.

A whale-sized woman opens her lexicon to me,
teaching new definitions of "cock" and "dick"
and translating "cunt" into spectacular poetry.
Next, a warrior resplendent in a feather headdress
invites me in the startlingly direct manner of his tribe
to be his *tayo*, or intimate male friend. As I explore
the deltas and jungles and inland seas of women's bodies,
several men join in, and soon all sexes are mingling
and merging in the polymorphous paradise of Polynesia.

Then one day in a moment of repose, I noticed
a girl whose nipples looked like firm, pink buds of flowers.
She stood in a corner, touching me only with her eyes,
and suddenly the frenzied orgies left me cold.
The slender maiden's name is Fayaway.
No words can describe the fragrance of her skin,
the sweet taste and texture of her private places,
the waves of ecstasy that surge along my spine
when I enter the tropical regions that lie
between her legs and linger long.
Here the delicious Latin words forbidden to me
when I was in school—words like *Vulva, Mons Veneris,
Vagina*—stay right on the tip of my
    Lingua: language, tongue.

Melville in the Enchanted Nursery

One mild Pacific day as we were cruising
past the low-shaded coves and islands of Sumatra,
where spice ships ply their trade through the China Sea,
I saw on the horizon rings of mist
sparkling and pluming in the noonday air,
fountains of silver spray.

We hit a lone bull, who dragged us, then broke free,
hurtling our boat between two basking whales
into a lagoon where I could see
suspended in watery vaults, a pod of whales,
great nursing mothers with their suckling calves.
My shipmates, harpoons dangling, stood transfixed
watching the baby whales draw from the milk
a spiritual sustenance as they gazed skyward.

The grand armada floats, and I float with them
as, buoyed by my body and cradled by one fluke,
my newborn tugs my breast and gulps his food,
cord slack between us, his eyes like pearly pools.

I am mother of milkiness, dalliance and delight.
Flanks brushing continents, I circumnavigate the globe
breaching whenever I feel the urge to fly,
shouting "Mammal, Mammal, Mammal!" at the sky.

Melville Aboard the Frigate *United States*

I stand here at the mast-head in a trance,
holding a shroud, half hidden by the sails
and swaying from side to side as in a dance.

Below me, prairie ponies seem to prance
through undulant grasses, flicking their white tails
as I gaze at the water in a trance.

Aloft, I can escape the tyrant's glance,
his orders and his floggings and the jails
where shackled sailors writhe in painful dance.

Daydreaming is my sole deliverance
from the harsh life a man-of-war entails,
so I stand at the mast-head in a trance

watching the seagulls flaunt their elegance
as, spreading their wings like milk-white sails,
they glide and dip and soar as in a dance.

Perched in the rigging, waiting for a chance
to spy the silvery jets of roving whales,
I stand here at the mast-head in a trance,
swaying from side to side as in a dance.

Melville Sails into Boston Harbor, (October 1844)

If monotheism
had begun
in Massachusetts

He would have said:
"Be still and know
that I am Cod."

Melville Makes Notes for His First Novel

Typee: Polyncsian word for "lovers of human flesh"

whihenies: girls who skinny-dip with sailors

tayo: a very intimate male friend

breadfruit: a native food that grows on trees

tappa: cloth Marquesan women make from leaves

tabu: an unwritten rule, or interdiction

white civilized man: the most ferocious animal on earth

cannibals: people who eat the flesh of other people,
      e.g., missionaries, slave traders, and literary critics.

Melville Ponders Sperm-Whale Vision

The sperm whale's eyes sit
sideways on his head
looking the other way.

On second thought,
what *other* way
when only double-consciousness

can hope to apprehend
reality?—Both/And—
not Either/Or.

I mean, one eye faces right,
the other left, and the front
of his head is a dead blind wall.

The whale butts his head
against your boat
because he cannot see.

When ships get in his way,
they sink: the whale regards them
as mere *jeux d'esprit.*

Melville Meets Nathaniel Hawthorne
at a Picnic on Monument Mountain

The wagon lurched up the old logging road,
and when the rocky track became impassable,
we clambered out and trekked the wooded trail
past streams and gorges, cooled by dense green leaves.

When a sudden shower drove us to a cave,
Dr. Holmes pulled two bottles of champagne
from his India rubber bag, and, half-intoxicated,
Hawthorne and I talked through the thunderstorm.

"Mr. Hawthorne," I said, "your stories weave a spell.
You've fathomed the darkness of the human soul."

"Your voyages," he replied, "have taken you to paradise.
Yet human nature—if I read you right—
seems much the same, whether savage or civilized."

"The human heart's an island in a sea
of savagery, Mr. Hawthorne. The cannibals I knew
behaved with more civility than average Christians,
who plunder the tropics, evangelizing and enslaving men.
We're cannibals all, except that civilized people clothe
their barbarities in pious platitudes. Your Puritans,
my missionaries: they suck the sweetness
from the marrow bone and spit back splinters."

It may have been the echo in the cave, or the champagne,
but Hawthorne's words and mine seemed one.
His talk, like his tales, dropped seeds into my soul.
When we strolled out into the sun,
his blue eyes shone like luminous lagoons.
We climbed to the top up steps of stone
that seemed the entrance to the Titans' temple.
Below the granite crags and open sky
the valley rolled, and north of me,
Greylock rose above the trees.
I scrambled out on an outcrop of rock,
that looked like the bowsprit of a ship,
playing at hauling ropes and spotting whales.
When I turned to scan the landscape on all sides,
I felt earth sway, its bent rim spin and swerve.

"Come aboard," I called, but Hawthorne turned quite pale.
"I think I'll take a dive," I teased, leaning out into open sky.

"You fool," he cried, "You'll kill yourself for sure."

Oceans of boulders rolled beneath my feet,
and for a moment, I was a fleck of foam
dancing on the surface of the sea.

Melville at Arrowhead

The house, full-rigged, pitches against the sky.
The cow lows, restless in the rain, and wanders home.
In the distance, Greylock looms above the mist,
clouds scud down the valley and flood the furrowed farm.

The cow steams in her stall; her black and white flanks,
coarse as Indian blankets, twitch and shiver.
As I feed her pumpkin, the horse snorts
and switches his tail, crunching dried-out hay.
The wind cracks its bony knuckles on the barn,
the old cow chews her cud complacently.

Galoshes sucking mud, beard soaked with brine,
I trudge back to the house, and from the porch I see
the hump-backed mountain breaching.

Melville Hitches Old Charlie to the Wagon

The problem of western philosophy, of course,
is that it puts Descartes before the horse.

Melville Overhears Gossip in Pittsfield, Massachusetts

Why does he wear that jacket?
Nobody in Pittsfield
wears green to go upstreet.

> The earth is my mother.
> She wove me this coat to disguise
> the stones inside my skin.

When will he cut his hair?
With that sunburn and scraggly beard
he looks like a savage.

> I am King of the Cannibals,
> a bone through my nose,
> my toothpick a harpoon.

Melville? Ain't he the fella
who bought Doc Brewster's farm?
He made anything of that old place yet?

> There can be no profit in a land
> where men stake claims on human flesh.
> What harvest can farmers reap
> from blood-soaked soil?

I watched him the other day
during Sunday services.
He didn't sing the hymns.

> At Pontoosuc Lake I saw a small perch
> belly-up on the sand, its sunspot grown dim,
> its silver scales sprouting mold.
> Man kills with one dry hand.

Why does he write so fancy
when a few plain words will do?
His books are botches.

> The sea is my father, writhing and tossing
> like a wounded whale. Fate tightens
> its tentacles, and I swim for open sea.
> My books are lifeboats.

Melville at His Writing-Desk

I feel the ends of my bones
against this stiff chair
as I sit hunched over foolscap
holding a dead feather in my hand.

I hear footsteps on the stair,
the careful placement of a tray outside my door.
Lizzie pauses to listen, then turns
and goes downstairs to stoke the fire.

I might as well join her there.
I have written nothing.
I have splinters in my eyes,
my back is sore.

The snow is so thick,
I cannot see Greylock.
My mind is a blank sheet of paper,
my spine in this hard wood chair
a rusty harpoon.

Lizzie Melville among the Cannibals: An Interlude

Sometimes I feel like a kitten caught in the drapes,
or a bat upside down under the eaves, wings furled,
taking short breaths so no one will notice me.
Hanging laundry, I hum chanteys I learned at school
until I see sails billowing over Boston Harbor,
and hear the tide turn with a rustle, then a roar.

Winter mornings, as I pump icy water into an old
bucket, I imagine I am running through the pastures
out behind the barn, fleeing the antimacassars and
the bric-a-brac gathering dust on the étagère.
I return to the kitchen and fill the copper kettle.
A few drops sizzle on the iron stove. I measure
Herman's coffee carefully. Then the family sails in,
Mother Melville in the lead. The oatmeal thickens.

After breakfast, I fly upstairs to tidy Herman's room,
then I attend to my own correspondence.
Today, my dear stepmother Hope inquires,
"What has become of the girl who used to dream
of chasing whales and the dashing young sailor
who promised to show her the South Seas?"
I reply, "She lives on an island surrounded by cannibals,
dearest Mother, sewing back the strings her husband
rips from his drawers each and every day."

Melville Meets Astronomer Maria Mitchell

Strange, how Nantucket women
    watch and wait

pacing their rooftop walks
    in worn-out shoes,

their men the sun and planets,
    they the watchful moons.

This woman lifts her eyes
    to drink the stars:

the sky is her husband;
    comets, paramours.

Melville Explains Why He Started Writing Poetry

While foolscap rolled out
    lank corpses bled to white
I swam in volcanic seas
    and tried to write

quill dipped in brine, a crippled bird
    I toiled
the prose was all blubber
    the black pots smoked and boiled

exhausted and drained
    I spat out lines alone:
cannibal crunching words
    of flesh and bone.

On His Way to the Holy Land, Melville Meets Hawthorne, now U.S. Consul in Liverpool, for the Last Time

I can tell he disapproves.
by the way he asks when
the rest of my luggage will arrive.
"Never," I say. "In this soft satchel
I carry all any bone-bag needs
to rattle through ancient deserts
trying not to step into
the camel dung of doubt."
He asks when I'll be back, and I say
"Never," then he falls silent, this friend
whose words I drank like wine.

He closes his office,
and we walk the beach a while,
hands in our pockets,
hair tossed by offshore winds,
tacking with words as though
thoughts were hidden shoals.
Out in the harbor
foghorns hoot like owls,
the steamer for Constantinople
chugs toward shore.
His blue eyes go slate
against the graying sky.

Back in his office, I give him
my passport to countersign.
"We are travellers," I say,
"adrift in foreign lands
where people chant prayers
in languages God can understand."

He folds up my passport
and hands it back to me.

Melville in the Holy Land

Cairo:
Flies on their eyes at noon,
blind beggars lean against the wall.
In the valley, the Pyramids
rise from ancient tombs
where pharoahs lie,
hands folded on jewelled chests,
waiting for the boat that will carry
them through the reeds
to a more surprising shore.

Jerusalem:
Lepers crowd the entrance
blocking light as I blindly
follow the worn marble stairs
into the Holy Sepulchre of Christ.
Dizzy with heat and stench,
I reach for the iron railing—
there is none.

Melville in Judea

The true pilgrimage never ends.
It takes you over the edge
of the known world
into deserts of broken stone
where Bedouins in tents
and women swathed in veils
watch from behind their eyes.

Melville Watches as New York's 20th Colored Regiment Marches by his House at 104 East 26th Street

Parade dress: creased trousers, snappy jackets,
union blue, white gloves and gaiters,
boots buffed to match the lustre of their faces,
rifles on their shoulders, heads held high,
eyes bright with revolutionary visions,
the Twentieth Colored Regiment struts by
on its way to warships waiting at the river
to transport them to southern battlefields.

People who live in the brownstones on our street
peer warily from behind their curtains, convinced
that black men, armed, will turn their guns
to the business of revenge for generations of iniquity.

These uniformed men march through sullied streets
where late the blood of black New Yorkers ran
as tigerish mobs of whites hung Negroes from lamp posts
and burned the orphanage for colored children.
So now the jagged wheel of history turns, and angels
black as gunpowder go forth to expiate the curse of Cain.

In Boston, black people are singing freedom songs
and dancing to washboards, fiddles, drums, and bones.

Melville Learns of Hawthorne's Sudden Death

They say words began haunting him,
that he dreamed whole novels
but couldn't remember how to write them down,
that his notebooks were nightmares,
that, wandering in a maze of monsters,
he dropped the thread. Perhaps he smelled
the sharp stench of the minotaur and figured
he could either let himself be killed
or kill the beast and let himself be doomed
to lie in the labyrinth beside a rotting corpse.
Newspapers report he was found in a hotel room
in Plymouth, New Hampshire, by his old friend
and fellow traveler Franklin Pierce.

Cause of death: unknown.

Melville Testifies at the Inquest for his Son Malcolm

That morning, before I left for work,
I told Lizzie to let him sleep. "Let him be late.
His boss will punish him. Then he'll mend his ways."
He'd been working in his uncle's insurance firm
since he was seventeen. Made his own money,
started staying out too late. Not a drinker or womanizer,
he just liked to see shows at nightclubs with his friends.
Started staying out late, and worrying his mother,
so I took away his key and locked the door at midnight.
Told him he could sleep on the steps for all I cared, but
Lizzie thought I was too hard on him; that night
she let him in at half past three.

Mackey joined the militia as soon as he turned eighteen.
He'd parade around in his uniform waving his gun
at Stanny and the girls, but they weren't afraid
of his shenanigans. He was always play-acting.
When I was laid up with sciatica, he dressed up
as Jack-the-Giantkiller to distract me from the pain—
roared so loud our Newfoundland
ran howling and hid behind the door.
He was always play-acting, always teasing me.
I'd come down from my study, and he'd pretend
I was invisible. "Where dat old man?" he'd ask,
and I would answer, "Here dat old man be!"

That evening I got home from work later than usual,
exhausted from inspecting bales and boxes
and filling out forms all day. Lizzie said Malcolm
hadn't come down all day, so I called up to him.
He didn't answer, so I raced upstairs.
Had to kick down the door to get into the room.

At first, I thought he was sleeping, his cheek
on the pillow, his hair soft and rumpled
as a child's, his uniform neatly folded
to keep the jacket and trousers pressed.
"Wake up, Malcolm!" I said, and when
he didn't move, I shook him and shouted,
"Stop it, Malcolm! This is no time for games."

It was then I saw the bloodstain on the pillow,
the wound in his temple, the pistol in his hand.
I waited for him to ask, "Where dat old man?"
so I could answer, "Here dat old man be."

Melville Wonders Why No One Heard the Shot

As I stormed across Madison Square,
pigeons flew up at me
flapping their dirty wings,
and later I would wonder
what sound the house had made
as I spent my customary day
inspecting ships for contraband,
making sure no one had smuggled in
anything dangerous—diseased plants,
French contraceptives, or a gun.

Melville Turns Sixty

Regrets coil themselves around my brain
like tentacles squeezing blood from memories,
wringing the living water from desire
raging in me like a hurricane, sweeping
hopes and dreams into the maelstrom
as my heart gulps air through gashes in its gills.

The whole man contemplates the faceless,
undulating krakens with equanimity, resisting
the lures of nihilism, death. The mutilated man
pursues the whale intent on his revenge,
his loves confounded, his passions agony,
his joy choked by the flat cold fish of fear.

Melville and George Orwell Take Refuge Inside the Whale

We had swallowed so much hypocrisy
our throats were raw. When we shouted
NO! out there, nobody heard.
In here, we can loosen our collars
and relax, lying back to admire the joists,
beams, rafters, ridgepoles of Leviathan.

"I'm no man's Jonah," says Orwell.
"This is just another foul-smelling cave to me."
But to me, the whale's belly is a cathedral
whose buttresses are bones.

"See this scar on my windpipe?
I squeaked like a rat when they hoisted me
onto the stretcher there in Catalonia.
Do you know what it's like being shot?
It's like being at the center of an explosion."

"When the whale slaps his titan tail
beside your boat, you think heaven's cracked.
The hemp smokes as it whizzes by, and when
the dart strikes the creature's flesh, he churns
the sea to bloody foam with his tormented flukes.
    —It's a hellish sight."

"I'm a landlubber," Orwell responds,
curling his lanky frame against the ribs.

"Have you ever," I ask, "seen a great beast die?"

He looks at me long and hard,
then spits out a reply:
"I have killed for a uniform
like your damned Captain Vere,
proving my potency on an aged elephant.
Some said the poor bugger was crazy,
but he was no crazier than the rest of us.
We went to India for glory, and ended up
grinding the ragged natives into the dust.
It's weak men turn to tyranny, you know."

I pull on my pipe and think of Ahab's quest,
the quest to destroy whatever teases Man:
mystery, magic, wonder, reverence, death.
Kill death before it kills us. Ignore the warnings,
prophecies and signs, and hunt—
like madness maddened—one pure doom.
"Apocalypse, " I say, and he responds:

"The Bomb in my day. You did it tribe by tribe,
but we learned to take the whole world down at once.
Radiation kills better than army blankets laced
with smallpox any day. We call it progress, old chap."

"In my day, progress meant new prisons and asylums
for widows and orphans, the indigent and insane.
Politicans and preachers extolled the Solitary System
and praised the architecture of The Tombs,
while in Florida, Seminole women and children
who survived the massacres were given castoff clothing
and exiled from their ancestral lands to North Dakota."

"In Burma, the kaffirs spat on our starched
white uniforms and jeered. Once I dreamt
that an Indian servant was laughing at me,
and when I looked at myself, I saw I was wearing
nothing but my spats and skivvies."

"It's a man-o'-war world," I say.
"In the Navy, they shave you with a rusty razor.
They crack your nuts and feed them to the sharks
I've seen men flogged until their skin hung in bloody strips.
They looked like fresh-flensed whales, or Negro slaves.
I can't see the red stripes on the flag without hearing
the screams of shipmates flogged until they fainted."

Orwell closes his eyes and leans back against the bones
"The bloke who created Man in His image
is a bloody incompetent sod,"

As I puff my pipe, the huge bowels rumble, and
the creature vomits both of us into the sea.

Outside the Whale, Melville Questions Salman Rushdie

Why couldn't *my* books have been banned?
Don't they deserve a death threat or two?
Why wasn't I forced into hiding, a price on my head
stores bombed for stocking *Moby-Dick*,
readers rushing to buy that wicked book
before the bookshops all burst into flames?

Melville Enjoys Late Reveries of Love

The aster blooms not where the tall palm grows
but bursts from brittle leaves and frost-glazed grass.

Now as the aster drinks the autumn sun
that warms the honeyed pastures, clover blooms,

and mingled with the lonely palm tree's sighs
I hear the soft, sweet whisper of the rose.

Melville Keeps on Writing

Like Beethoven deaf and stranded
      in silences so savage
the bones of his skull could sing

I too am "held back by Art,"
      its terrible silences
its fierce and blinding beauty.

Acknowledgments

Igitur; rivista annuale de lingue, letterature e culture moderne, ed. Gordon Poole. "Melville at his Writing Desk," "Melville Explains Why He Started Writing Poetry," "Melville Meets Nathaniel Hawthorne at a Picnic on Monument Mountain," and "On His Way to the Holy Land, Melville Meets Hawthorne, Now U. S. Consul in Liverpool, for the Last Time."

Leviathan: a Journal of Melville Studies, ed. John Bryant. "Melville Explains Why He Started Writing Poetry" and "Melville in the Holy Land" (as "Melville Visits Sacred Cities").

October Mountain: An Anthology of Berkshire Writers, ed. Paul Metcalf. "Herman Melville, an Aging Customs Inspector, Reminisces."

Poetry Online. "Melville at Arrowhead," "Melville Heads for the Pacific aboard the *Acushnet,*" and "Melville Ponders Sperm-Whale Vision."

Radcliffe Quarterly, ed. Ruth Whitman. "Melville Discovers an Enchanted Nursery."

Sad Little Breathings and Other Acts of Ventriloquism, ed. Heather McHugh. "Melville Ponders Sperm-Whale Vision."

Sandscript, ed. Jean Lunn. "Melville at His Writing Desk," "Melville Meets Astronomer Maria Mitchell on Nantucket," and "Melville Arrives in the Marquesas" (as "Melville Swims toward Marquesan Maidens").

Scripsit, ed. William Sutton: "Melville Meets Hawthorne at a Picnic on Monument Mountain" and "Melville Receives the News of Hawthorne's Death."

The North American Review, ed. Vince Gotera. "Melville Continues His Classical Education in the South Seas."

The Worcester Review, ed. Rodger Martin. "Melville Continues His Classical Education in the South Seas" (with the permission of The North American Review), and "Melville Overhears Gossip on Pittsfield's Main Street."

I am grateful to the editors who published these poems, the wonderful friends who encouraged and put up with me all these years, and the fine poets who inspired and critiqued my work: the late Ruth Whitman for introducing me to persona poetry, Michelle Gillett, Julia Thorne and Wendy Mnookin for their sustained friendship and invaluable advice, Stephen Tapscott for his early recognition of my work, Everett Hoagland and Elizabeth Schultz for their abundant generosity of word and spirit, and Kathleen Spivack for her exquisitely tough mentoring and commitment to her craft.

Thanks also to the Breadloaf Writers' Conference, the Virginia Center for the Creative Arts, and Künstlerhaus Schloss Wiepersdorf for granting me space and time to work on these and other poems in beautiful places that offered both isolation and the fellowship of other artists. I also want to thank Lou Esposito and Michael Steinman at UMass Dartmouth for awarding this book a Provost's Subvention Grant.

Finally, I want to say how grateful I am to the folks at Spinner Publications: Joe Thomas for taking on this project and designing the handsome layout and typography, Andrea Tavares for being so patient, vigilant, and good-natured with my endless tinkering, Jay Avila for creating such a gorgeous cover, and Claire Nemes for her expertise in preparing the cover copy.

About the Author

Laurie Robertson-Lorant is the author of *Melville: A Biography,* the only up-to-date, full-length, fully annotated, complete, one-volume biography of Melville. After teaching at Berkshire Community College, St. Mark's School, Southborough, School Year Abroad, France, and MIT, Dr. Lorant is currently a Full-Time Visiting Lecturer at UMass Dartmouth. Her poems have appeared in the *Atlanta*

Guido Röger photograph

Review, Birmingham Poetry Review, Black Buzzard Review, Earth's Daughters, Igitur, Intuitions, Leviathan, Oxalis, Radcliffe Quarterly, Rockhurst Review, Sandscript, Scripsit, Sing, Heavenly Muse, Southcoast Poetry Journal, The American Voice, The North American Review, and *The Worcester Review,* and in several anthologies: *October Mountain: An Anthology of Berkshire Writers,* edited by Paul Metcalf, *Sad Little Breathings* and *Other Ventriloquisms,* edited by Heather McHugh, and *We Speak for Peace,* edited by Ruth Jacobs.